World Almanac® Library of American Immigration

German
Americans

Michael V. Uschan

Curriculum Consultant: Michael Koren,
Social Studies Teacher, Maple Dale School, Fox Point, Wisconsin

WORLD ALMANAC® LIBRARY

Dedicated to the students and teachers at Raymond Elementary School.

Please visit our web site at: www.garethstevens.com
For a free color catalog describing World Almanac® Library's list of
high-quality books and multimedia programs, call 1-800-848-2928 (USA)
or 1-800-387-3178 (Canada). World Almanac® Library's fax: (414) 332-3567.

Library of Congress Cataloging-in-Publication Data

Uschan, Michael V., 1948-
    German Americans / by Michael V. Uschan.
        p. cm. — (World Almanac Library of American immigration)
    Includes bibliographical references and index.
    ISBN-10: 0-8368-7310-6 — ISBN-13: 978-0-8368-7310-8 (lib. bdg.)
    ISBN-10: 0-8368-7323-8 — ISBN-13: 978-0-8368-7323-8 (softcover)
    1. German Americans—History—Juvenile literature. 2. German Americans—
Social conditions—Juvenile literature. 3. Immigrants—United States—History—
Juvenile literature. 4. Germany—Emigration and immigration—History—Juvenile
literature. 5. United States—Emigration and immigration—History—Juvenile
literature I. Title. II. Series.
    E184.G3U73   2007
    973'.00431—dc22   2006005319

First published in 2007 by
World Almanac® Library
A member of the WRC Media Family of Companies
330 West Olive Street, Suite 100
Milwaukee, WI 53212, USA

Copyright © 2007 by World Almanac® Library.

Produced by Discovery Books
Editors: Jacqueline Gorman and Clare Weaver
Designer and page production: Sabine Beaupré
Photo researcher: Rachel Tisdale
Maps and diagrams: Stefan Chabluk
Consultant: Maddalena Marinari
World Almanac® Library editorial direction: Mark J. Sachner
World Almanac® Library editor: Barbara Kiely Miller
World Almanac® Library art direction: Tammy West
World Almanac® Library production: Jessica Morris

Picture credits: Cincinatti USA Regional Chamber/Paula Norton: 42; CORBIS: /Bettmann
18, 23; /Underwood and Underwood 31; Getty Images: /Three Lions 8 (bottom); /MPI
11 (top); Byron Collection/Museum of the City of New York 11 (bottom); /Hulton Archive
19, 24; /George Eastman House 21; /Jacob A. Riis/Museum of the City of New York 28;
/Keystone 34; /Fred Ramage 35; /Gene Lester 37; /Mark Wilson 40; The Granger
Collection, New York: 26; Library of Congress: title page; 5, 8 (top), 20; /Doris Ullman
15; /Brady-Handy Photograph Collection 32; The New York Public Library, Astor, Lenox
and Tidlen Foundation: cover; 12; Topfoto: /Bob Daemmrich/The Image Works 29;
/Syracuse Newspapers/The Image Works 41.

Printed in the United States of America

1 2 3 4 5 6 7 8 9 10 09 08 07 06

Contents

Front cover: A German family is inspected on arrival at Ellis Island immigration station in New York Harbor in the early 1900s.

Title page: Horse-drawn wagons transport kegs of beer at the Joseph Schlitz Brewing Company, Milwaukee, Wisconsin, 1900.

Introduction

The United States has often been called "a nation of immigrants." With the exception of Native Americans— who have inhabited North America for thousands of years— all Americans can trace their roots to other parts of the world.

Immigration is not a thing of the past. More than seventy million people came to the United States between 1820 and 2005. One-fifth of that total—about fourteen million people—immigrated since the start of 1990. Overall, more people have immigrated permanently to the United States than to any other single nation.

Push and Pull

Historians write of the "push" and "pull" factors that lead people to emigrate. "Push" factors are the conditions in the homeland that convince people to leave. Many immigrants to the United States were—and still are—fleeing persecution or poverty. "Pull" factors are those that attract people to settle in another country. The dream of freedom or jobs or both continues to pull immigrants to the United States. People from many countries around the world view the United States as a place of opportunity.

Building a Nation

Immigrants to the United States have not always found what they expected. People worked long hours for little pay, often doing jobs that others did not want to do. Many groups also endured prejudice.

In spite of these challenges, immigrants and their children built the United States of America, from its farms, railroads, and computer industries to its beliefs and traditions. They have enriched American life with their culture and ideas. Although they honor their heritage, most immigrants and their descendants are proud to call themselves Americans first and foremost.

Welcome to the United States

Willkommen is the German word for "welcome," and German immigrants have been welcomed to the United States since the 1600s, when they first began leaving their homes in Europe to venture bravely to the New World. A unified German nation did not exist until 1871, so the area from which Germans came changed over time. Throughout those four centuries, however, Germans came for the same reason people from around the world have always immigrated to the United States—they wanted a better life.

From 1820 to 1924, 35.9 million people came to the United States. Of this total, about 16 percent were German—a higher percentage than any other single ethnic group. In all, more than 7.2 million Germans have immigrated to the United States. In the 2000 U.S. Census, more than 42.8 million people—approximately one in six Americans—claimed that their ancestors had been German. That is the largest group of Americans to claim ancestry from a single country or ethnic group.

▲ Santa Claus in a Civil War cartoon of 1863 by German immigrant Thomas Nast.

German Traditions That Became U.S. Traditions

Two figures that U.S. children know and love—Santa Claus and the Easter Bunny—have German origins. German immigrants brought with them the tradition of St. Nicholas, who it was believed distributed gifts to good boys and girls each year on December 6. In 1823, the popular poem "A Visit from St. Nicholas" (often now called "The Night Before Christmas") by Clement Clark Moore changed the date of the visit to Christmas Eve. St. Nicholas also became known as Santa Claus after *Sinterklaas*, the Dutch version of St. Nicholas. During the Civil War, a cartoon by German immigrant Thomas Nast created the image we have today of Santa Claus (*see picture above*). In Germany, the Easter Bunny was known as *Osterhase*, a magical rabbit that, on the night before Easter, laid candy eggs that children joyfully hunted for on Easter. These characters were created in Germany to help celebrate the Christian holy days of Christmas and Easter. In the United States, Santa Claus and the Easter Bunny have become part of the nonreligious traditions surrounding those holidays.

CHAPTER 1

Life in the Homeland

In 1753, Johannes Schlessmann sent a letter to relatives in Germany explaining why he was so happy that he and his family had immigrated to America. Schlessmann wrote, "I and my children and my wife thank and praise God a thousand times, that we are in this healthful country. We expect to support ourselves much better here than in Germany, for this is a free country."

Schlessmann's letter summed up the two main reasons that some seven million Germans came to the United States: the opportunity to better themselves economically and the chance to have more freedom. Like other Germans, Schlessmann left his homeland because he had struggled to make enough money to survive there and hated living under a system of government that would not allow him to have basic rights.

Unhappy in Their Homelands

Germany did not become a unified nation until January 18, 1871, when about three dozen individual states in the area that today makes up Germany banded together to form the German Empire. From the 1600s through 1870, Germany had been divided into many small states, some the size of a single city. The people in those states shared a common language—German—and traditions and beliefs that should have united them.

Some of those states (such as Prussia, Bavaria, and Hesse) were ruled by members of nobility or royalty, including kings, queens, and princes. These rulers governed selfishly and made life difficult for average people. The rulers taxed the people heavily so they themselves could live richly. One German man wrote his ruling prince that he was leaving for America because "I do not know how to make ends meet here anymore." Royal families also owned nearly all the land, including farms. People who worked on farms

◀ This map shows Germany and its neighboring countries as they are today. There wasn't a unified German nation until 1871.

were peasants, who were paid little, had few rights, and were never allowed to leave their jobs. Many Germans moved to America so they could own their own land.

Royal rulers held complete power over their subjects. They could imprison people for any reason and steal their possessions. They could also force people to join an army to fight a war. Rulers also controlled the religion their subjects could follow. Many Germans fled their homeland because they wanted the freedom to worship as they chose.

> "There were nine children in the family, five of them boys. If we stayed, they might be drafted in the next war, and be shot to death for the King and the Fatherland. Father had been a soldier himself, and he did not want that fate for his sons."
>
> *Ernst Bohning, explaining that his father brought the family to the United States in 1843 so that his sons would not be forced to join the army and fight a war*

Religious Conflict

In 1618, Roman Catholics and Protestants in European nations such as France and Spain began fighting an armed conflict known as the Thirty Years War. This war was fought mostly in the area known today as Germany. Before it ended in 1648, with a peace treaty that let individual nations (but not necessarily individual people) choose their religion, an estimated thirteen million Germans had died from battle wounds, starvation, and illness.

In the 1600s and 1700s, the members of different Protestant denominations in Germany argued over the correct way to

▲ Market Place in Germantown, Pennsylvania, as recorded in a nineteenth-century print. Germantown was the first permanent German settlement in North America.

worship God, sometimes even beating and killing each other. Smaller religious groups like the Mennonites, Amish, and Moravians were persecuted because their beliefs were different from those of other Protestants.

When members of the persecuted groups fled Germany, many emigrated to the British colony of Pennsylvania in North America. They chose it because William Penn, the colony's governor, had promised religious freedom to people of any faith. This freedom was unusual during a time when most nations, and even some British colonies, formally recognized only one branch of Christianity.

On October 6, 1683, the ship *Concord* docked in Philadelphia, Pennsylvania, with thirty-three Mennonite immigrants from Krefeld, Germany. Under the leadership of Francis Daniel Pastorius, they established the first permanent German settlement in North America: Germantown. Pastorius praised Governor Penn for allowing Mennonites to have religious freedom even though Penn was a Quaker, a different Protestant denomination: "[He] has granted to every one free and untrammeled exercise of their [religious] opinion, and the largest and most complete liberty of conscience."

▲ An elderly Mennonite woman reads from an eighteenth-century Moravian bible in 1950.

Gemütlichkeit in German Life

Although conditions in their former homeland had often been hard, German immigrants never forgot the enjoyable aspects of life in what they fondly referred to as the Old Country. These happy occasions were summed up by the German word *Gemütlichkeit*, which has several meanings ranging from "hospitality" to a general philosophy that people should try to enjoy life. Gemütlichkeit helped Germans bring some fun and enjoyment into lives that were often filled with hardship.

From the nineteenth century onwards, as their communities grew, German Americans practiced Gemütlichkeit in many ways. They listened to music, especially German composers such as Ludwig van Beethoven, Richard Wagner, and Johannes Brahms, who wrote some of the world's most memorable music. Germans also loved to sing and dance. Even small communities had choirs that performed on special occasions. At weddings and on holidays, people performed traditional folk dances as well as newer German dances, such as waltzes and polkas.

Many Germans were also passionate about nature. After visiting Germany, Englishman Hewitt Williams wrote a book in 1842 in which he proclaimed that "Sunday is their great out-of-doors day." Williams said that individuals and entire families took long walks in the forests that surrounded their communities. They also had picnics, rowed on lakes, and took part in other activities to enjoy their homeland's natural beauty. Sunday leisure activities were among the many traditions that Germans would bring to America.

Who Was a German Immigrant?

Germany did not exist as a unified nation until 1871. It is difficult, therefore, to label any one group of immigrants arriving before that date as German. In general, immigrants before 1871 were considered German if they spoke German in their native land and shared traditions and customs with other German-speaking people. A German immigrant, then, could be someone from neighboring Austria as well as groups of Germans who lived in parts of Switzerland, Luxembourg, Bohemia, Poland, Hungary, and Russia. Thus, a common language and cultural heritage, not the particular nation someone came from, defined who was a German immigrant to America.

CHAPTER 2

Emigration

The history of German immigration to the United States is old and rich. Germans, in fact, were among the first to visit the future nation's easternmost and westernmost shores. When Norwegian explorer Leif Ericson traveled to the east coast of North America sometime after the year 1000, one of his crew members was a German named Tyrker. In January 1778, when English explorer Captain James Cook became the first European to discover the Sandwich Islands (which later became the Hawaiian Islands and, in 1959, the fiftieth U.S. state of Hawaii), his crew included three German sailors.

Germans were also some of the first permanent settlers of the land that would become the United States. Jamestown, Virginia, the first permanent British colony, was founded in 1607. When seventy new colonists arrived there a year later, eight of them were skilled German workers—three carpenters who could build houses and five glassmakers. Captain John Smith, the colony's leader, praised the Germans for helping Jamestown to grow and contributing to its development.

Another early German arrival was Peter Minuit, who in 1626 became governor of New Netherland, a colony the Netherlands (also known as Holland) had established in 1624. Minuit gained everlasting fame when he bought the island of Manhattan from the Man-a-hat-a Indians for goods— glass beads, colored cloth, kettles, and small mirrors—estimated to be worth just

"Hail to you, future generations in Germanopolis! May you never forget that your ancestors, of their own free will, left the beloved land, which bore and nourished them [to] live the rest of their days in the forests of Pennsylvania, in the lonely wilderness, with less care and anxiety, but still after the German fashion, like brothers. May you also learn, how arduous a task it was [to] plant the German race in this part of North America."

Francis Daniel Pastorius, who helped found Germantown, Pennsylvania in 1683, in a message to future German newcomers

◀ Three ships lie at anchor at Jamestown, Virginia, the first permanent English settlement in North America in a painting from 1610. Skilled German workers (carpenters and glass-makers) who arrived in 1608 helped to build Jamestown.

a few dollars. The island was taken over in 1674 by the British and today is the richest borough of New York City.

Coming to America

Even though Germans have been coming to the United States for four centuries, it has always been hard for emigrants to bid farewell to their friends and relatives—certainly harder than leaving their homeland itself, because conditions there were so difficult. John Schuette moved to Wisconsin in 1848. Years later, he remembered how sad his family, their friends, and their relatives had been the day the emigrants began their long journey to their new home. "Tears flowed in profusion," Schuette said. "Anyone leaving for America was considered as about to pass into eternity [die]."

The loved ones left behind felt as if the emigrants were dying. They knew that after these family members sailed to a land thousands of miles across the Atlantic Ocean, they would probably never see them again. During the first three centuries of German emigration, there was also the very real danger that the immigrants might actually die during the journey itself.

Most German immigrants departed from the busy ports of Bremen and Hamburg. Although their favorite destination was Philadelphia, Germans landed at ports spread along the eastern

▶ Emigrants heading for New York huddle in blankets outdoors on board ship, 1893.

▲ A German family photographed in the early 1900s at Ellis Island, the point of arrival in New York City.

"During the voyage there is on board these ships terrible misery, stench, fumes, horror, vomiting, many kinds of seasickness, fever, dysentery, headache, heat, constipation, boils, scurvy, cancer, mouth rot, and the like, all of which comes from the old and sharply salted foods and meat, also from very bad and foul water, so that many die miserably."

Gottlieb Mittelberger, describing his 1750 journey to the United States

coast, from New York City all the way south to New Orleans, Louisiana on the Gulf of Mexico. Until the end of the nineteenth century, when steam-powered ships made the crossing faster, easier, and safer, the voyage across the Atlantic was dangerous and extremely uncomfortable. Passengers were crowded into the holds of sailing ships where they encountered cramped quarters, dirty conditions, and poor or spoiled food.

The sea trip could take several months. In 1750, one ship needed six months to cross the ocean because heavy storms continually slowed the vessel during a long and difficult journey. Angela Heck remembered how frightened passengers were when a storm struck the ship carrying her and her husband Nikolaus in 1854: "We thought the ship would be ripped apart at any moment. . . . We repented our sins, and we all prepared to die."

Emigrants did die when ships sank in storms. Even more passengers became sick or died from diseases like typhus that were caused by filthy living quarters on board, where people used buckets as toilets and had little water to wash themselves. Thousands of Germans died during the trips to their new homes. In 1732, three Germans complained in a letter about the terrible conditions that killed one hundred of the 150 people aboard the ship *Love and Unity*. Most died because the ship's food supply ran out. "To keep from starving," they wrote, "we had to eat rats and mice."

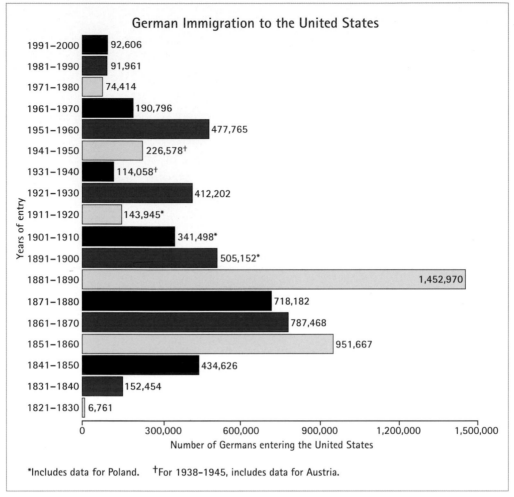

German Immigration to the United States

Years of entry	Number of Germans entering the United States
1991–2000	92,606
1981–1990	91,961
1971–1980	74,414
1961–1970	190,796
1951–1960	477,765
1941–1950	226,578†
1931–1940	114,058†
1921–1930	412,202
1911–1920	143,945*
1901–1910	341,498*
1891–1900	505,152*
1881–1890	1,452,970
1871–1880	718,182
1861–1870	787,468
1851–1860	951,667
1841–1850	434,626
1831–1840	152,454
1821–1830	6,761

*Includes data for Poland. †For 1938–1945, includes data for Austria.

Source: U.S. Citizenship and Immigration Services, 1821-2000

⏶ This chart shows the number of Germans arriving in the United States, 1821–2000.

Waves of Immigration

The difficulties and dangers of the journey, however, did not stop Germans from coming to America. It is estimated that as many as one hundred thousand Germans immigrated to the North American British colonies before 1775, when colonists began the American Revolution to win independence from England. By 1790, about 277,000 German immigrants and their descendants lived in the United States, 7 percent of the nation's population.

Most of the early German immigrants came because of religious persecution at home. Pennsylvania guaranteed people religious freedom and, in 1790, it was home to about 225,000 residents of German ancestry. Many were Mennonites, who in 1683 had founded Germantown, the first permanent German settlement in the

The Pennsylvania Dutch

When German immigrants began settling in Pennsylvania in 1683, they became known as the "Pennsylvania Dutch" even though they were not from the Netherlands, where people are called Dutch. English-speaking colonists in Pennsylvania called the newcomers "Dutch" because of confusion over the German word Deutsch, which means "German." When the Germans said they were "Deutsch," their new neighbors thought they meant "Dutch." This nickname was mistakenly applied to many other German immigrants. The term is still used today by the Pennsylvania Dutch because of tradition. The customs and habits of the Pennsylvania Dutch were similar to those of other Germans when they arrived in America. In the years since then, many Pennsylvania Dutch have not adapted to modern ways and do not, for example, use electricity or cars.

United States. Although many of the early immigrants from other countries were single men, Germans tended to come as families because they were all endangered by persecution.

During the Thirty Years War, one German state, called the Palatinate, suffered more than any other state. To escape the war's devastation, an estimated fifteen thousand Lutherans and other Protestants from the Palatinate fled, first to Holland and then to England. The British sent most of them to colonies in North America. In 1708, a small group settled in New York's Hudson River valley and established Neuburg, a city known today as Newburgh. In 1714, more Palatines founded Germanna in Virginia.

A great wave of German immigration began after 1848, when social revolutions swept across the German states. The people wanted to bring democracy to states still controlled by royalty, but they failed. Thousands of people who supported the revolts, who became known as Forty-Eighters, moved to the United States to gain political and social freedom—freedom they had long sought and that people in the United States had long enjoyed. Many did so, however, with a heavy heart. John Kerler, who immigrated to Wisconsin in 1849, wrote home that he had wanted to remain in Germany, but because of "the threatening prospect for the future of [freedom in Germany for] religion and politics, I prefer America."

During the 1850s, nearly one million Germans came to the United States, including more than 220,000 in 1854 alone. Even more Germans came in the 1880s, when almost 1.5 million made the journey. They included Catholics who were fleeing religious persecution that started after Germany was unified in 1871 and the Protestant religion was established as the new nation's preferred religion.

German Jews

From 1830 to the 1880s, another group fleeing religious persecution—Jews—swelled the numbers of German immigrants to the United States. A wave of anti-Semitism forced tens of thousands of German Jews to leave their homeland. German states passed laws in the early nineteenth century that denied Jews many rights, including the right to own land or hold certain jobs, and some German citizens beat and murdered Jews in vicious riots.

▲ Albert Einstein in 1931, two years before he left Nazi Germany for the United States.

Although anti-Semitism eased in the late 1800s, German Jews had to fear for their lives again in 1933 when Nazi leader Adolf Hitler came to power. In the six years before Hitler started World War II in 1939, Jews were viciously persecuted by the Nazis and thousands of German Jews fled to the United States. Thousands of Christian intellectuals and political opponents of the Nazis also left Germany to avoid being jailed or killed. The most famous refugee was Albert Einstein, the brilliant Jewish scientist who emigrated to the United States in 1933.

Although about 130,000 German Jews found safety in the United States in the 1930s, U.S. immigration officials denied permission to thousands of other Jews. In 1924, the United States had set annual quotas for immigrants from each country. U.S. officials refused to waive the quotas to admit more German Jews (or Christians) even though their lives were in danger.

One of the cruelest rejections came in 1939, when Representative Robert Wagner of New York introduced a bill in Congress to allow twenty thousand German Jewish children to enter the United States. The measure was voted down, leading journalist Dorothy Thompson to write, "It is a fantastic commentary on the inhumanity of our times that for thousands and thousands of people a piece of paper [a visa] is the difference between life and death." Many of the children denied entry were among the six million Jews the Nazis killed in the Holocaust. When the United States did finally admit more Jews, in general, the more educated were allowed in most easily.

Arriving in the United States: 1700-1900

German immigrants have generally been welcomed to the United States. They integrated more easily than many other ethnic groups for a number of reasons. The United States and American society were still in formation when the first Germans arrived, so German customs were more easily adopted. Germans also shared a religion—Christianity (and especially the Protestant denomination)—with many other European immigrants, and a similar cultural background. In the 1700s, when the majority of U.S. settlers were English, this bond was especially strong because the English kings were partly German due to marriages between the English and German royal families.

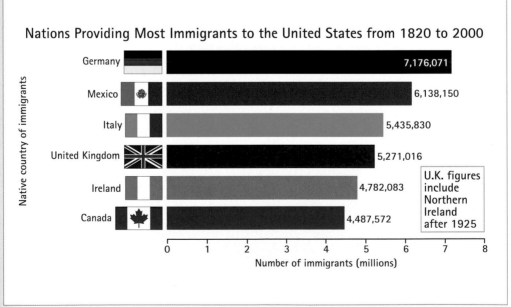

Nations Providing Most Immigrants to the United States from 1820 to 2000

Native country of immigrants	Number of immigrants (millions)
Germany	7,176,071
Mexico	6,138,150
Italy	5,435,830
United Kingdom	5,271,016
Ireland	4,782,083
Canada	4,487,572

U.K. figures include Northern Ireland after 1925

Source: U.S. Citizenship and Immigration Services, 1820-2000

▲ The nations that have provided the most immigrants to the United States are shown in this chart. More people have come from Germany than any other nation.

Germans were also accepted in the early years of the United States because they had skills the young nation needed. Although like most colonists, many Germans became farmers, German glassmakers, printers, beer brewers, sausage makers, gunsmiths, and other workers provided vital services and products that helped the colonies grow and made life better for their people. An example of how warmly German Americans were accepted is the praise that Dr. Benjamin Rush (a signer of the Declaration of Independence) lavished on them in his 1789 book, *An Account of the Manners of the German Inhabitants of Pennsylvania*. Most Germans who settled in Pennsylvania were farmers, and Rush said their agricultural skills and love of hard work helped the state become a good place to live. He also complimented the Germans for being "kind and friendly as neighbors."

In many ways, then, German immigrants had an easier time adjusting to life in the United States than immigrants from other countries. Even immigrants who were welcomed, however, still faced difficulties in making a new life in the United States. For some, adjusting to life in their new homeland was extremely hard.

Indentured Servants

Immigrants who were too poor to pay for their passage had the toughest time. They came to the United States as indentured servants. To pay for their trip, they had to work for someone without being paid for as long as seven years. The length of their service depended on the terms of a contract they signed. Parents sometimes even had to sell their children as indentured servants, because they had not been able to pay for the children's passage to the United States.

Indentured servants were similar to slaves. They could not quit their jobs or move. Their employers controlled their lives in many ways, including deciding

"Many parents must sell and trade away their children like so many head of cattle, for if their children take the debt upon themselves, the parents can leave the ship free and unrestrained; but as the parents often do not know where and to what people their children are going, ... after leaving the ship, [they] do not see each other again for many years, perhaps no more in all their lives."

Gottlieb Mittelberger, a German who lived in the United States from 1750 to 1754, describing how German children were sold as indentured servants when they arrived in Philadelphia

▲ Henry Villard, a highly successful German-born publisher.

whether they could marry or have children. During the term of their service, however, indentured servants often acquired valuable skills that helped them find good jobs when their debt was paid. Before 1820, about half of German immigrants came as indentured servants.

Even German immigrants who arrived with no debt, however, had some problems. The circumstances facing eighteen-year-old Ferdinand Hilgard when his ship docked in New York City in 1853 was typical. Hilgard had no money, knew no one, and "to crown all," he wrote years later, "I could not speak a word of English." When another immigrant loaned the desperate young man twenty dollars, Hilgard was able to begin making a new life for himself. He changed his name to Henry Villard to make it sound "American" and moved to Milwaukee, Wisconsin, where he became a journalist. Villard eventually became a successful financier and publisher who owned the *New York Evening Post* newspaper and *The Nation,* America's oldest continuously published weekly magazine.

The German Roots of English

Most German immigrants learned English easily because many words in English and German are similar. English itself is derived from an ancient form of German spoken by Germanic people who settled England in the fifth and sixth centuries. In fact, an estimated 60 percent of English words are derived from German. The following words, for example, are quite similar in both languages: *Vater* (father), *Mutter* (mother), *Wasser* (water), *Ding* (thing), *Hilfe* (help), *Sohn* (son), *Licht* (light), and Buch (book). Some German words that immigrants brought to the United States were incorporated into the English language. They include kindergarten (meaning "children's garden"), frankfurter and wiener hot dog), and Gesundheit (health), which many people say to wish good health to someone sneezing.

▲ The *Staats Zeitung* (a German-language newspaper) building in New York, 1895.

Most Germans quickly picked up the new language when they arrived because of similarities between German and English. Many immigrants lived in communities, however, where they could continue speaking German every day because so many other German immigrants lived there, too.

German Communities

Like other immigrant groups, Germans arriving in the United States often settled near each other. They were frequently drawn to such areas by "America letters" that earlier immigrants sent back to Germany, praising their new homes. Germans also tended to band together so they could share the cultural traditions they loved. They could speak German and read German newspapers, and they formed associations and clubs. In addition, newcomers could expect help from Germans who had immigrated before them.

Most German immigrants wanted to marry people from their own country. Because more single men than single women immigrated from Germany, the men often wrote letters seeking brides from their homeland. Descendants of German immigrants, however, often married people from other countries and religions. Exceptions are members of the Amish and Mennonites, whose religious and social beliefs gradually separated them from other groups of people. They always chose to marry people from their own groups. If they

▲ Kegs of beer being transported on horse-drawn wagons at the Joseph Schlitz Brewing Company, Milwaukee, Wisconsin, 1900.

"As far as I am concerned, I can, hand on heart, declare naught else but that I thank the Lord that I am here and regret that I did not come sooner; and when my memory turns to many among you and I reflect how, with your means, you could live here, I am sorry, humanly speaking, not to have you here."

Johann Friederich Diederichs, who moved to Wisconsin with his wife and four children in 1848, in an "America letter" to friends in Germany urging them to emigrate

did not, they risked being excluded from their communities.

Large German populations grew in cities such as Cincinnati, Ohio; New York City; Chicago, Illinois; Milwaukee, Wisconsin; St. Louis, Missouri; and Fredericksburg, Texas (which was named after a German prince), and their presence shaped many communities. Milwaukee, for example, became known in the nineteenth century for holding many German cultural events. The city owed much of its early prominence to beer makers such as Frederick Pabst, Joseph Schlitz, and Frederick Miller. In 1893, Pabst Brewing Company became the first in the United States to sell more than one million barrels of beer in a single year.

German brewers also helped transform the social life of their communities by opening "beer gardens" where people could listen to music and dance.

German Pioneers

Although many Germans flocked to big cities, some enjoyed the challenge of being pioneers and helped expand the nation's boundaries by moving to unsettled wilderness areas. One such pioneer was Emma Murck Altgelt, who immigrated to New Braunfels, Texas in the middle of the nineteenth century after a relative wrote how wonderful the state was. "Texas became the land of my dreams," said Altgelt. New Braunfels was settled in 1845 by German prince Karl of Solms-Braunfels, and Fredericksburg, Texas, was settled a year later. Both communities played an important role in settling some of Texas's wide open spaces.

In Germany, most immigrants had worked as farmers on land owned by the rich. In the wilderness areas of the United States, land was cheap—sometimes even free—and for the first time, Germans could own their farms. They used their skill in growing crops such as potatoes and wheat and raising livestock such as dairy cattle to become successful farmers. A favorite destination for German immigrants in the 1840s was the Midwest, where they helped settle and create states that included Wisconsin, Minnesota, North Dakota, and South Dakota.

When Germans moved to such wilderness areas, they had to clear land for farms and build their own homes. In places where there was timber, these were usually one-room log cabins. On the prairie where timber was scarce, however, houses were made out of sod (soil with grass and roots attached). Anton Senger, who immigrated to North Dakota in 1886, remembers how frightened he was to have only a sod shack to protect his family during a terrible three-day blizzard. "We used hay for fuel and that soon gave out . . . all we could do was sit inside and try to keep from freezing," he wrote.

When they were able to build nicer homes, immigrants often made them in the German half-timbered style. This design conserved lumber by filling in exterior space with bricks and stones that were then covered with plaster. Germans had used this method to build houses in Europe where lumber had been scarce for centuries.

▼ German settlers standing in front of their Midwest sod homestead, around 1880.

Building a Nation: 1700-1900

In 1854, Father Ambrose Oschwald and 114 other immigrants arrived from Baden, Germany, to settle St. Nazianz, Wisconsin. The Catholic priest saw their new home as a place of refuge for Roman Catholics fleeing religious persecution. "We did not come to America to become rich," Oschwald said, "but to save our souls." The dream of wealth, however, attracted many Germans. One woman told *Independent* magazine that she immigrated to the United States in the late 1800s because "I heard about how easy it was to make money in America and became very anxious to go there."

No matter what pulled Germans to the United States, the result has been the same for four centuries: They have helped to build and shape their adopted homeland.

Creating the Colonies

Germans helped establish the United States by taming what was then a vast, unknown wilderness. This was a hard job for people who came from Europe, which had been settled for centuries.

In 1714, when German immigrants founded Germanna in Virginia, it was the westernmost settlement in the British colonies. A year later, Englishman John Fontaine described the primitive conditions in which the Germans lived. He said the nine homes they had built were surrounded by a tall wooden stockade, which they needed for protection against attacks by wild animals or Native Americans. (Some Native people resented people living on land that had been theirs for many centuries.) Near the homes inside the stockades were wooden sheds for hogs and other farm animals. "The Germans live very miserably," wrote Fontaine. The hardships such immigrants endured, however, helped them create rural communities that became the backbone of future states such as Pennsylvania, Virginia, and North Carolina.

German craftsmen brought skills that made life easier for the colonists and helped the colonies grow economically. In 1690, Wilhelm Rittenhaus established the first paper mill in the colonies in Germantown, Pennsylvania. In 1716, Thomas Ruetter founded the first ironworks at Matawny Creek in Berks County, Pennsylvania. In 1738, Kaspar Wüster started the first large-scale glass factory near Salem, New Jersey.

Another significant event during the colonial period occurred in 1743 when Christopher Saur of Philadelphia printed a copy of the bible in German—the first bible printed in the New World in a European language. Saur also published a German newspaper, and by the mid-1700s, every large city had at least one German-language newspaper.

The Trial of John Peter Zenger

Another printer was John Peter Zenger, a German immigrant who helped establish an important freedom for people in the United States. When Zenger arrived in New York as a thirteen-year-old in 1709, he was an orphan because his father had died on the voyage from Europe. In 1733, after learning the trade of printing as an apprentice, Zenger began publishing the *New York Weekly Journal.* The newspaper ran stories that criticized William Cosby, the governor of the colony of New York. One article claimed that Cosby had illegally tried to influence elections for the Assembly, the legislative body that made New York's laws.

Cosby was so angry that he had Zenger arrested on November 17, 1734. Zenger was charged with libel for publishing critical statements about Cosby. (At the time, libel meant publishing any damaging statements, whether true or false.) Although

▲ The burning of Zenger's *New York Weekly Journal*, Wall Street, November 6, 1734.

Zenger remained in jail for eight months, his wife, Anna, and others continued printing the newspaper.

Zenger's trial was held in August 1735, and jurors found him innocent after deciding that the stories about Cosby were true and that the paper had the right to criticize the governor. When the Bill of Rights—the first ten amendments of the U.S. Constitution—went into effect in 1791, one of the most important new safeguards for citizens was freedom of the press. Gouverneur Morris, who helped write the Constitution, credited Zenger with establishing that right: "The trial of Zenger in 1735 was the germ of American freedom, the morning star of that liberty which subsequently revolutionized America," Morris said.

Germans in the Revolutionary War

Many German Americans took an active role in the American Revolution. On July 4, 1776, representatives of the thirteen colonies met in Philadelphia, where they approved the Declaration of Independence. The first story about the historic document appeared in the *Philadelphia Staatsbote*, a German newspaper. Most of the estimated one hundred thousand German Americans backed the Revolution. They were quick to support the fight against England even though England's king was of German heritage. A main reason they had left their own countries was the way royalty had mistreated them by denying them equal rights and limiting their opportunities. Thus, they had no sympathy for a country ruled by a king who imposed his will on people several thousand miles away.

▲ Baron Friedrich Wilhelm von Steuben, a German soldier who trained the Continental Army in the Revolutionary War.

Molly Pitcher

Although women were not allowed to serve as soldiers in the American Revolution, a few did fight for their country. The most famous was Maria Ludwig Hays, who is better known in history as "Molly Pitcher." Like many other wives, this daughter of German immigrants went to war with her husband, John, to clean and cook for him. At the Battle of Monmouth in New Jersey on June 28, 1778, she earned her nickname by braving enemy fire to bring pitchers of water to thirsty soldiers. When her husband was wounded, she also helped fire his cannon. To reward her valor, Pennsylvania in 1822 granted her an annual pension of forty dollars.

Some American colonists went to war carrying a gun developed by German Americans—the Pennsylvania Rifle—that was better than the weapon used by British soldiers. German gunsmiths in Pennsylvania were the first colonists to make gun barrels with spiral grooves, a technique called rifling. Guns with rifled barrels could shoot bullets farther and more accurately than smooth-barreled muskets, the weapons British soldiers had. German soldiers were usually the Continental Army's finest shooters.

The best-known German American military figure was Baron Friedrich Wilhelm von Steuben, who trained Continental soldiers. A professional soldier, von Steuben was made a general by the Continental Army even though he did not speak English (he used interpreters). Historians claim von Steuben improved the army's fighting ability with the drills and discipline he taught the soldiers.

Heading West

In 1790, most U.S. residents lived in the original thirteen states along the Atlantic Ocean. In the next one hundred years, however, people would push the nation's borders west to the Pacific Ocean across a vast, unknown wilderness.

Of the thousands of German Americans who participated in this historic westward expansion, none played a more vital role than immigrant Johann Augustus Sutter. Born in Germany in 1803, Sutter came to the United States in 1834. In 1839, when he settled in California, the future state was then a Mexican province.

▲ This painting of the 1850s shows settlers in a Conestoga wagon heading for a new life in the western states.

"Every night the wagons were ranged in a wide circle, the animals placed within to prevent stampedes or their being run off by the Indians or molested by wild beasts. . . . Wild animals abounded, particularly coyotes, and buffaloes ranged the plains in countless numbers. . . . Our fuel consisted of 'buffalo chips' [dried buffalo and cattle dung], which lay everywhere in greatest profusion."

Samuel J. Kline, the son of German Jewish immigrants, describing his family's trip by wagon train from Kansas to Denver, Colorado

Mexican officials gave Sutter 50,000 acres (20,000 hectares) of land at the junction of the American and Sacramento rivers. When gold was found at Sutter's Mill in August 1847, the discovery touched off a mad rush for riches that within a decade brought nearly four hundred thousand new residents to California. Among them was Levi Strauss, a German Jewish immigrant who became rich making canvas pants for miners. More than 150 years later, people still wear Levi jeans.

The Gold Rush helped ignite a wave of migration by millions

"Before the children went to school in the morning and after they returned in the afternoon, they had to help with the regular chores. They fed the . . . cows, horses, hogs, chickens, dogs, and cats; they milked the cows, rounded up and counted the sheep in the afternoons, gathered the eggs, chopped and brought in stove wood. The girls worked in the kitchen and garden."

Gilbert C. Jordan, the son of German immigrants, describing the many tasks children had to do on the family farm in Texas

of settlers to western areas such as California (which the United States gained control of in 1846). They made the long, difficult journey in Conestoga wagons designed by German Americans in Pennsylvania. The heavy wagons with flapping canvas tops—which were 25 feet (7.6 meters) long and 11 feet (3.3 meters) high to the top of the wagon cover—could hold 3 tons (2.7 metric tons) of cargo. Conestogas carried German Americans and other settlers across the United States, helping create new states such as Wisconsin, Minnesota, North Dakota, South Dakota, Arizona, Colorado, and Washington.

Texas, which became a state in 1845, was a popular destination for German immigrants. Some settled in communities that were mainly German, such as New Braunfels and Fredericksburg, while others spread out into different areas. The hardy pioneers who went to Texas found that life was not easy. When Rosa Kleberg and her family moved to Texas in 1834, her brothers thought they could spend most of their time hunting and fishing. "It was hard for them," she wrote, "to settle down to the drudgery and toil of splitting rails [to make fences] and cultivating the field, work which was entirely new to them."

Germans in the Civil War

Westward expansion was temporarily halted in 1861 by the Civil War, the conflict that nearly split the United States in half. When the war began, more than 1.3 million German Americans lived in the United States, more than 4 percent of its total population of 31.4 million.

One of the main causes of the conflict was slavery. Most German Americans backed the northern states and federal government during the Civil War because they opposed slavery. Most had left Europe to come to the United States because they had lacked freedom in the Old Country. Well into the nineteenth century, workers had been treated almost as property by those who employed them. Slavery reminded many immigrants of the conditions in their homeland, and they opposed it. In fact, the first Americans to oppose slavery formally were the people of Germantown, Pennsylvania, who in a town meeting on February 18, 1688, claimed it was wrong for people to own other people.

During the Civil War, many Germans became war heroes, including Carl Schurz, August Willich, and Franz Sigel. While German Americans fought on both sides, the vast majority were Union soldiers.

Bringing Germany to America

Westward expansion in the United States resumed after the Civil War ended with a Union victory in 1865. Millions of Germans came to the United States in the late 1800s—almost 1.5 million arriving during the 1880s, the peak decade of German immigration. Many joined the westward push across the continent.

▲ Children at a summer school kindergarten class in Brooklyn, New York, 1902.

▲ Brass band concerts are a German tradition brought to the United States by German immigrants and still enjoyed today.

German Americans in the late 1800s began to influence U.S. life still further. One of their most important contributions was to help shape the U.S. education system, which became modeled after Germany's structure of elementary schools, high schools, and universities. Schools today still use the German word kindergarten—which means "garden of children"—to refer to the first year of elementary school. Margaretha Meyer Schurz started the first U.S. kindergarten in 1856 in Watertown, Wisconsin. Germans also introduced physical education classes to schools. The U.S. tradition of free public schools meant that immigrant children could become educated even if their parents were poor. The free schooling through high school and often affordable college education helped

German Americans, over time, to get better jobs than their parents, and improve their social and economic skills.

German Americans also influenced social life and appetites. Most people in the United States now enjoyed eating German foods such as frankfurters (hot dogs) and sauerkraut and drinking German beer. By the 1870s, the nation had four thousand breweries, most of them run by Germans. This adoption of German tastes was most evident in cities like Cincinnati, Ohio, and Milwaukee, Wisconsin, which, by 1900, had populations that were more than 50 percent German or of German descent. German immigrants introduced others in the United States to organized, outdoor leisure activities on Sundays, such as band concerts and picnics. Germans also persuaded many cities to begin the local and state park systems that Americans still enjoy using today.

Socialism and Unions

Germans helped shape U.S. political thought. Many Germans believed in socialism, a political and economic philosophy that claims the public should own and benefit from land, factories, and other property that produces wealth. Socialism is opposed to capitalism, the accepted system in the United States, under which individuals own most property.

In 1867, German immigrants in New York City started the nation's first Socialist party. Although Socialists were never influential at the national level, many were elected to local office. Milwaukee had many Socialist mayors, the best known of whom were Daniel Hoan and Frank Ziedler. They served for a total of thirty-six years. The Socialist belief that a nation should use its wealth to help its citizens influenced the development of twentieth-century federal programs such as Social Security and Medicaid.

Germans also played key roles in creating the labor movement to secure good pay and conditions for workers. One immigrant, Oscar Ameringer, joined the *Deutsche Holz Arbeiter Verein* (German wood workers' union). The union was part of the Knights of Labor, an early national workers organization. Ameringer remembered protesting with other workers to limit the work day to eight hours. "We just marched and marched and sang and sang," he said.

The march failed, but unions in the twentieth century, led by German Americans such as Walter Reuther, won higher pay and better and safer working conditions for millions of people.

▲ German and Russian immigrants wave flags at the arrival of President Theodore Roosevelt in Victoria, Kansas, 1903.

Germans From Russia

Some nineteenth-century German immigrants actually came from Russia. After Catherine the Great became empress of Russia in 1762, she promised Germans free land and religious freedom if they settled in Russia. She did this because she was German herself. Although Germans prospered at first in Russia, they began fleeing that country in the mid-1800s when the Russians became hostile to them. The Germans were especially angry that the Russians were forcing young Germans to serve in the army. When thousands of Germans who lived in Russia came to the United States, they entered as Germans and not Russians.

Challenges of the Twentieth Century

Like other immigrants, most Germans wanted to become good citizens by learning to speak English and adopting U.S. customs and ideas. They also wanted, however, to retain the rich heritage of their former homeland by speaking German (at least among themselves) and enjoying Old Country foods, music, and dances such as the polka and waltz.

In a speech at the Chicago World's Fair in 1893, Carl Schurz explained that German immigrants had to balance those two conflicting desires so that they could be good Americans. "It means," said Schurz, "that our character should take on the best of that which is American, and combine it with the best of that which is German."

Schurz was an example of how that could be done. After coming to the United States in 1852, he fought in the Civil War, published a German newspaper in St. Louis, and was elected to the U.S. Senate. For other German Americans, though, this balancing act became increasingly difficult in the twentieth century when their adopted homeland fought their old nation in two major wars.

◀ Carl Schurz, as Senator of Missouri, around 1870.

World War I

German immigrants had generally faced little discrimination in the United States. This changed dramatically for the country's twelve million citizens of German ancestry in 1917, when the United States entered World War I against Germany (three years after Germany began the war in 1914). The wartime hatred that the United States felt for Germany and its citizens was also directed at German Americans in the United States. Anyone with a German-sounding name like "Fritz" or "Schmidt" was called "Hun,"—an offensive term for a German. People who spoke German in public were beaten. This even happened to a Lutheran pastor in Corpus Christi, Texas who delivered his sermon in German. In one terrible incident, on April 5, 1918 in Collinsville, Illinois, a mob hanged a German immigrant named Robert Prager for not enlisting in the U.S. armed forces. In fact, Prager had tried to join the navy but was rejected.

Irrational mobs burned German books, destroyed German music (including works by Beethoven), and changed German words to erase them from the country's vocabulary. In the United States, people now ate "liberty cabbage" (instead of sauerkraut) and "liberty sausages" (instead of frankfurters), became sick with "liberty measles" (rather than German measles), and walked "liberty dogs" (not dachshunds). Even President Woodrow Wilson cast doubt on the loyalty of German Americans when he said that the hyphen—as in "German-American"—was "incompatible with patriotism." Although Wilson was also referring to immigrants from other countries that were Germany's allies in the war, such as Austria, Hungary, and Czechoslovakia, German Americans suffered the worst from wartime intolerance.

The fears about German Americans were misguided. At first, some German Americans had backed Germany in war. When the United States declared war on Germany, however, all but a few German Americans were loyal to their adopted homeland, and hundreds of thousands of German Americans fought for the United States.

▲ Henry Kissinger, photographed here in the early 1970s, was a Jewish immigrant who left Nazi Germany and later became a prominent U.S. government official.

New German Refugees

German immigration increased in the two decades after World War I ended in 1918. In the 1920s, more than four hundred thousand Germans immigrated because the war's devastation and continuing economic problems made life in Germany very difficult. These new immigrants settled in larger cities rather than rural areas because there were now more jobs in factories and other industries.

People began leaving Germany in the 1930s for a different reason—they were frightened by racial hatred. When Adolf Hitler and his Nazi Party gained control of Germany in 1933, Jews began leaving because Hitler hated Jews and had vowed to eliminate them. Many non-Jewish intellectuals, artists, and political leaders also left because they feared that life under a dictator like Hitler would be unbearable. About 114,000 Germans emigrated to the United States during the 1930s (when it became difficult to get permission to leave Germany) up to 1939, when World War II began with Hitler's invasion of Poland.

Jewish immigrants included Albert Einstein, one of history's greatest scientists, and fifteen-year-old Henry Kissinger, who became a top U.S. official and in 1973 shared the Nobel Peace Prize for helping to end the Vietnam War. The fears that German Jews had were real. During the Holocaust, Hitler killed six million or two-thirds of European Jews. Although some managed to escape from Europe or survive the Holocaust, the vast majority did not.

World War II

When the United States entered World War II in 1941, some German Americans suspected of being loyal Nazis were arrested. There was no repeat, however, of the widespread discrimination of World War I because German Americans had proven their loyalty by fighting against Germany in that war. During World War II, most German Americans hated Hitler as much as everyone else.

During the war, nearly one-third of the sixteen million U.S. soldiers who fought were German Americans. Among them was Kissinger, who served as an infantry soldier. Most famous was General Dwight D. Eisenhower, who was the top commander for all Allied troops in Europe. Eisenhower played a key role in defeating Hitler's powerful army. In 1953, he became the United States' second German American president. (The first was Herbert Hoover, who served from 1929 to 1933.)

Another immigrant who made an important contribution to the war effort was actress Marlene Dietrich. Born in Berlin, Dietrich moved to Hollywood, California in the 1930s to make films and became a U.S. citizen in 1937. Because she hated what Hitler had done to her homeland, Dietrich worked hard to help her adopted country win the war. She sold a record number of government war bonds and entertained U.S. troops overseas, sometimes in places so close to enemy lines that she was in danger. When high-ranking

▼ German-born actress Marlene Dietrich signs autographs for U.S. soldiers in Germany. She made many trips overseas to entertain U.S. troops in World War II.

officers asked the famous star why she risked her life, she replied in German, "*aus Anstand*," which means "it was the right thing to do."

Postwar Immigration

Germany was defeated in 1945. Afterward, nearly seven hundred thousand Germans immigrated to the United States in the 1950s and 1960s. They came because life was difficult in Germany, whose economy had been shattered by the war. Many also fled because their homeland had been politically divided into two parts, East and West Germany. West Germany was a democracy, but East Germany was communist and controlled by the Soviet Union.

Many Germans sought sanctuary in the United States because they did not want to live under communism. Among them were scientists like Werner von Braun, who had developed deadly rockets that Germany had used to attack England during the war. Although Von Braun and other German scientists could have been arrested as war criminals for having been members of the Nazi Party and because slave labor had been used to build the rockets, the U.S. government welcomed them because it needed their expertise to stay ahead of the communists technologically. In fact, in a controversial move, the U.S. government negotiated for the immigration of important Nazi German scientists before the end of World War II, so that they would not end up working for the Russians. In the United States, von Braun used his rocket knowledge to develop the space program. His crowning achievement came on July 16, 1969, when the crew of *Apollo 11* landed on the Moon.

German American Achievements

Von Braun was one of many German Americans whose accomplishments have significantly strengthened, shaped, and enriched their adopted homeland. They have included businesspeople, artists, athletes, scientists, and two presidents—Hoover and Eisenhower.

One of the first German American millionaires was John Jacob Astor, who built a fur-trading empire in the 1800s that stretched across the country and helped open the west to settlers. Brewers like Frederick Pabst and *würstmacher* (sausage maker) Fred Usinger helped change U.S. tastes, and their products are still sold under their names today. Other successful businessmen include timber baron Frederick Weyerhaeuser, and John Jacob Bausch and Henry Lomb, who manufactured optical products.

◀ Theodor Geisel, better known as Dr. Seuss, with a copy of his book, *The Cat in the Hat*, 1957.

Entertainment owes a huge debt to German Americans as well. In 1888, the five Ringling brothers bought their first elephant and began the Ringling Brothers Circus, which made circuses popular. In 1912, film pioneer Carl Laemmle cofounded Universal Pictures, which has since produced thousands of movies. There have been hundreds of German American actors, including current stars Leonardo DiCaprio, Sandra Bullock, and Kirsten Dunst, whose father was born in Germany.

German American writers John Steinbeck and Kurt Vonnegut wrote influential novels, while Theodor Geisel (better known as Dr. Seuss) penned children's classics that will live forever. Cartoonist Thomas Nast (who came to the United States as a child) was the first to draw the political character Uncle Sam, while Charles Schulz created the beloved comic strip *Peanuts*. Among leading sports stars are Olympic swimmer Johnny Weissmuller, who later starred in *Tarzan* movies, and baseball greats George Herman "Babe" Ruth and Lou Gehrig.

The Katzenjammer Kids

Katzenjammer is a German word for the yowling noise cats can make. It is also part of the title of the historic, influential comic strip *The Katzenjammer Kids*. German immigrant Rudolph Dirks began drawing it in 1897 for the *New York Journal*, and a version produced by Hy Eisman still appears in newspapers today. The comic centered on two mischievous German children, Hans and Fritz, and the adults they annoy with their pranks, including Mama, the Captain, and the Inspector. Dirks's strip was the first to use balloons to represent characters' thoughts and speech. Hans and Fritz were among the characters featured on U.S. stamps in 1995 that honored a century of comic strips.

CHAPTER 6

German Americans in U.S. Society

The discrimination German Americans faced in World War I led many of them to abandon their ethnic heritage. Fearing they would no longer be accepted by their fellow citizens, some tried to become more "American" by changing their names from "Heinz" to "Henry" or "Schmidt" to "Smith." Others quit speaking German, even at home, and concealed their ancestry in other ways. Herbert Hoover's original family name—which was changed before he was born—was Huber. When he successfully ran for president in 1928, he was careful not to mention that he was German American.

Any lingering effects of anti-German prejudice from World War I disappeared when German Americans again helped their adopted nation in World War II. In the decades since then, German Americans have once again become free to show pride in their ethnic heritage. Their adopted country has even set

[The U.S. flag] "passed by the rows of silent people—the men with their hats over their hearts, the women standing very straight and quiet, the children saluting. It was a hushed, almost reverent moment, a time of great emotion for all of us. I have often thought that those immigrant farmers, most of whom could not even speak English, were probably the most American Americans I have ever known."

Bandleader Lawrence Welk, one of the most popular television stars of the 1950s, remembering the patriotism of German Americans during the Fourth of July parade in his boyhood home of Strasburg, North Dakota

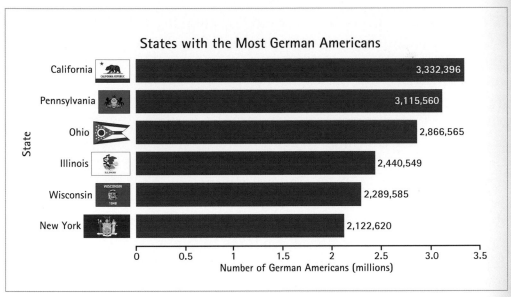

States with the Most German Americans

State	Number of German Americans
California	3,332,396
Pennsylvania	3,115,560
Ohio	2,866,565
Illinois	2,440,549
Wisconsin	2,289,585
New York	2,122,620

Number of German Americans (millions)

Source: U.S. Census Bureau, Census 2000

▲ This chart shows the states where the greatest number of German Americans live.

aside one day each year to honor them and their ancestors for the contributions they have made to the United States.

Honoring German Americans

Every October 6 is German American Day. President Ronald Reagan proclaimed the first one in 1987 to honor the 304th anniversary of the 1683 arrival in Philadelphia of immigrants from Krefeld, Germany. (Although other Germans had already come to America, these immigrants established Germantown, the first permanent German settlement.) In proclaiming the first German American Day, Reagan noted that there were more Americans of German ancestry than any other single nationality. He also praised German Americans for helping to make the United States the richest and most powerful country in the world.

The proclamation filled every German American with pride even though most no longer spoke the language, engaged in traditional German activities such as folk dancing, or had active ties to the Old Country. Many German Americans, however, still find many ways to celebrate their heritage.

Still German and American

The Web site for the German-Texan Society in Austin, Texas, greets visitors with a hearty "Guten Tag Y'all." The German words for

"Good Day" coupled with the southern phrasing for "you all" is a whimsical blending of German and American cultures. The words are also important symbolically because the Web site greeting shows how German Americans, even in the twenty-first century, have managed to fit into U.S. culture while retaining a sense of pride in their heritage. In the nineteenth century, so many Germans settled in Texas that they began to influence the development of the young state's emerging culture. One of the most lasting contributions of this infusion of German culture can be seen today in Tejano music, which is a blend of traditional Mexican styles and German music. Tejano music contains rhythms similar to the polka, the lively German folk dance. And one of the most distinctive Tejano musical instruments is the accordion, which Germans brought with them from the Old Country.

In the 2000 U.S. Census, nearly 43 million people identified themselves as German Americans. In 2004, it was estimated that 1.4 million people speak German at home. Among them are members of Amish and Mennonite religious groups who still cling to the past in many ways, including shunning general use of modern technology such as automobiles and electricity. Many of the four hundred thousand U.S. high school students who study German

▲ A horse-drawn carriage carrying two Amish women in Maryland, 2005. The Amish reject modern-day conveniences, such as automobiles, and so still use horse-power.

▲ Hot dogs are one of the lasting German contributions to American food.

each year—it is the third most popular foreign language taught, after Spanish and French—do so to honor their German ancestors.

People interested in German culture or news from Germany can read German-language newspapers printed in the United States like Chicago's *Amerika Woche* (American Week) or the bimonthly magazine *German Life*. In addition, cities with large German American populations have groups that help people learn to perform traditional songs and dances or speak German.

The easiest way in which German Americans continue to show the pride in their heritage is to eat traditional foods, either at German restaurants located in every major city, or at home from family recipes handed down from generation to generation. Eating traditional foods is a fairly private way to celebrate their German ancestry, but there are many ways today in which German Americans can publicly display a love for their cultural heritage.

Celebrating Their Heritage

As the bitterness toward Germany began to fade in the 1950s, German Americans began displaying their cultural pride more openly. Some of the first events were called German Days or Steuben Days. They were both held on September 17, the birthday of Baron Friedrich Wilhelm von Steuben, who had helped the United States win its independence during the American Revolution.

▲ Traditional German folk dancing on display at the Oktoberfest in Cincinatti, Ohio.

Since the 1950s, there has been a dramatic increase in the number of events honoring German culture and German American achievements. Most of them are U.S. versions of Oktoberfest, the traditional festival held in October in cities across Germany to celebrate the fall harvest. German Americans, however, also flock to events like Wurstfest, held each November in New Braunfels, Texas, where some Texans trade their cowboy boots and hats for lederhosen, the traditional short leather pants worn in Germany.

The largest annual display of German American pride is German Fest, a three-day celebration held each July in Milwaukee. This nationally acclaimed festival attracts tens of thousands of people who come to savor bratwurst and beer and listen and dance to polka music.

The German American Legacy

An event like German Fest can appeal to Americans from many different ethnic backgrounds. German immigrants continued so many of their customs in their adopted homeland that they are familiar to other Americans. Nearly everyone enjoys eating a frankfurter, and many in the United States know that when they use words like kindergarten or Gesundheit, they are actually speaking German.

Millions of Americans even live in communities whose names reflect German American heritage. Bismarck, North Dakota is named for Otto von Bismarck, who helped unite Germany and was its political leader in the late 1800s. Although Bismarck is the only state capital named for a German ruler, almost every state has a city named Berlin (the German capital) or some variation of it, like New Berlin or East Berlin.

The legacy of German Americans, however, is much greater than mere place names. In proclaiming German American Day on October 6, 2005, President George W. Bush said that Americans are indebted to German immigrants for helping create the nation in which they live. Bush said that the millions of German immigrants who came to the United States in search of religious freedom and economic opportunity not only helped found the country but also helped to ensure that others would have the same opportunities in the future. "German Americans," said the president, "have played an important role in establishing America as a land where liberty is protected for all of its citizens."

After four centuries, Germans are still immigrating to the United States in search of a better life. In 1989, the communist regime in East Germany fell, leading to the reunification of East and West Germany in 1990. Germans living in East Germany, who had not been allowed to leave the country, could now live anywhere they wanted. For many, the choice was the United States.

Preserving the Schuhplattler Dance

Perhaps the best-known German folk dance is the *Schuhplattler*, a spirited number in which men dressed in lederhosen (short leather pants) hop and twirl around madly while slapping the bottoms of their shoes. Groups across the country are working to teach German Americans such dances so they will not die out in the United States. One of the groups is the Alpentänzer Schuhplattler of Sacramento, California. (*Alpentänzer* means "Alpine dances.") The group is trying to preserve not only German and Austrian folk dances like the Schuhplattler, but the costumes and culture surrounding them. In 2005, this group had forty dancers as well as a live band, the Alpen Tanz Kapelle. It performed authentic German dances throughout California and the Reno and Tahoe area of Nevada in an attempt to keep this vibrant part of German culture alive in the United States.

Notable German Americans

John Jacob Astor (1763–1848)
Businessman who came to the United States at the age of twenty to sell musical instruments but became rich selling furs that his company bought throughout the continental United States. He also made a fortune in real estate in New York City.

Albert Einstein (1879–1955) Jewish physicist considered the twentieth century's greatest scientist, he came to the United States in 1933 after Adolf Hitler's rise to power. A letter he wrote to President Franklin D. Roosevelt led to the development of the atomic bomb, which helped the United States defeat Japan in World War II.

Henry Kissinger (1923–) Secretary of State under President Richard Nixon and co-winner of the 1973 Nobel Peace Prize. Born Heinz Alfred Kissinger in Fuerth, Germany, his Jewish family fled Nazi persecution in 1938.

Thomas Nast (1840–1902) Political cartoonist who came to the United States at the age of six. He created the images of Santa Claus, Uncle Sam, and the Democratic Party donkey and Republican Party elephant symbols.

Francis Daniel Pastorius (1651–1719)
Leader of the group of Mennonites who moved to Pennsylvania in 1683 seeking religious freedom and who founded Germantown, the first permanent settlement of German immigrants in America.

Carl Schurz (1829–1906) Political leader who, after immigrating to the United States in 1852, fought in the Civil War, published a German newspaper, and served as a U.S. senator and secretary of the interior. His wife, Margaretha Meyer Schurz, started the first U.S. kindergarten in 1856.

Friedrich Wilhelm von Steuben (1730–1794) Professional German military officer who helped teach the colonial Continental Army the basics of military drill and discipline during the American Revolution.

Levi Strauss (1829–1902) German Jew who immigrated to the United States in 1847 and in 1853 opened Levi Strauss & Co. in San Francisco, California. He became rich by selling rugged canvas pants, which became known as Levis, to gold miners.

John Peter Zenger (1697–1746)
Printer who came to America as a thirteen-year-old in 1709. He helped establish the right of freedom of the press during a trial in 1735 after he printed newspaper articles critical of New York's colonial governor.

Time Line

1608   Eight skilled German workers arrive at the British colony of Jamestown, Virginia.

1618–1648   Roman Catholics and Protestants in Europe fight the Thirty Years War in the area known today as Germany.

1683   October 6: Thirteen families of German Mennonites seeking religious freedom found Germantown, Pennsylvania, the first permanent German settlement in America.

1735   German immigrant John Peter Zenger is found innocent in a historic trial that establishes the principle of freedom of the press.

1777   Friedrich Wilhelm von Steuben, a professional German soldier, begins training the Continental Army.

1790   An estimated 277,000 people of German ancestry live in the United States.

1845   New Braunfels, Texas, is established by 150 German families.

1847   Gold is discovered at Sutter's Mill in California, sparking the Gold Rush.

1848   Social revolutions sweep across the German states. When they fail, the thousands of people who supported the revolts (known as "the Forty-Eighters") immigrate to the United States.

1856   German immigrant Margaretha Meyer Schurz establishes the first U.S. kindergarten in Watertown, Wisconsin.

1867   German immigrants in New York City start the nation's first Socialist party.

1871   January 18: Some three dozen individual states in the area that today makes up Germany band together to form the German Empire.

1880s   In this decade of the greatest German immigration, nearly 1.5 million Germans come to the United States.

1914–1918   World War I is fought (United States involved from 1917–1918); many German Americans are discriminated against.

1933   Many intellectuals, scientists, and Jews begin fleeing to the United States after Adolf Hitler and his Nazi Party assume control of Germany.

1939–1945   World War II is fought (United States involved from 1941 to 1945); approximately five million German Americans fight with the U.S. military.

1987   October 6: President Reagan declares the first German-American Day.

1990   East and West Germany are reunified; many emigrate from East Germany.

2000   In the U.S. Census, nearly 42.8 million people, 15.2 percent of the nation's population, claim German ancestry.

2004   An estimated 1.4 million U.S. residents speak German at home.

Glossary

ancestry the country or countries one's ancestors came from

anti-Semitism prejudice against Jews

apprentice young person who works, usually for free, for a skilled person to learn a trade or craft like printing

capitalism a political system under which wealth or assets, such as land and factories, belong to private individuals rather than the government

census official population count

colony nation, territory, or people under the control of another country

communist political system in which the government has strong control and property is shared among all citizens

Continental Army the colonial army that fought against the British during the American Revolution

culture language, beliefs, customs, and ways of life shared by a group of people from the same region or nation

denomination particular Christian religion, such as Catholic or Baptist

emigrate leave one nation or region to go and live in another place

Forty-Eighters people who supported the German revolutions of 1848

Gemütlichkeit a German word that means "hospitality" and generally expresses the joy of life

heritage something handed down from previous generations

Holocaust systematic murder of six million Jews by Nazi Germany and its allies during World War II

immigrant person who arrives in a new nation or region to take up residence

immigrate to arrive in a new country to live

indentured servant worker who agrees to work for no salary for a set period of time to pay off a debt, such as for his or her passage to America

libel to print false accusations about someone

Old Country the affectionate term German immigrants had for their homeland

peasant person of low social status who generally worked on farms

persecute to treat cruelly and unfairly

Protestant member of a non-Catholic Christian church, such as the Lutheran, Episcopalian, Methodist, or Presbyterian churches or the Church of England

quota assigned proportion; in the case of immigration, a limit on the number of immigrants allowed from a particular country

Socialist an economic system under which members of society collectively own and control the production of some goods and services

union organization that campaigns and negotiates for better working conditions for its members

visa document that permits a person to enter a nation for a set period of time

Further Resources

Books

Galicich, Anne. *The German Americans.* The Immigrant Experience (series). Chelsea House, 1996.

Hoobler, Dorothy, and Thomas Hoobler. *The German American Family Album.* The American Family Albums (series). Oxford University Press, 1996.

Sandler, Martin W. *Immigrants: A Library of Congress Book.* HarperCollins, 1995.

Schouweiler, Thomas. *Germans in America.* In America (series). Lerner Publications, 1994.

Web Sites

German-American Corner: History and Heritage
www.germanheritage.com
Biographies of German Americans, historical essays, statistics, and links to many other resources.

The Germans in America
www.loc.gov/rr/european/imde/germany.html
U.S. Library of Congress Web site with includes a time line and history of Germans in the United States.

Publisher's note to educators and parents: Our editors have carefully reviewed these Web sites to ensure that they are suitable for children. Many Web sites change frequently, however, and we cannot guarantee that a site's future contents will continue to meet our high standards of quality and educational value. Be advised that children should be closely supervised whenever they access the Internet.

Where to Visit

Pennsylvania German Cultural Heritage Center
Kutztown University
P.O. Box 306
Kutztown, PA 19530
Telephone: (610) 683-1589

About the Author

Michael V. Uschan has written more than fifty books and has twice won the Council for Wisconsin Writers Juvenile Nonfiction Award. Uschan lives in Franklin, Wisconsin. His grandparents were all immigrants to the United States from Austria.

Index